CW00539201
Bath to Baghdad

Bath to Baghdad

ELLEN TANNER'S COLLECTION OF MIDDLE EASTERN ART

CATRIN JONES

THE
HOLBURNE
MUSEUM

DIRECTOR'S FOREWORD

Most museum collections are rich repositories of many varied stories. The main narratives of the Holburne's are of Georgian Bath and of Sir William's nineteenth-century collecting. Perhaps the most intriguing of the untold stories is that of Miss Ellen Tanner, articulated through the collection of Persian artworks she bequeathed to the Holburne between the wars.

I am delighted to welcome this book, which has been published in celebration of the recent restoration of Miss Tanner's collection. After decades in storage the treasures that she bought in the Middle East have been brought back to life. This has been made possible through a fundraising campaign under the auspices of the Big Give Christmas Challenge, an imaginative initiative by which charitable gifts are match-funded to double the donation. I am very grateful indeed to the Big Give for this magnificent support, and to The Reed Foundation and others close to the Museum who pledged to match donations made to our public fundraising campaign. The success of that campaign, which exceeded its target of £50,000, is testament to the way in which Ellen Tanner's story captured all of our imaginations. I would like to thank each and every one who responded to our plea for support.

At the Holburne, I would like to thank our Curator, Catrin Jones, for championing the Tanner collection and for leading this project. She has been supported by Kate Vandor, who has joined the Holburne thanks to a grant from the Traverse Trust. The entire team contributed to the success of the fundraising campaign but I should single out for special thanks Jane Ibbunson, Oliver Merchant and Carol Hunt of our Development team. We benefitted greatly from the guidance of Alex Chapman, to whom I am very grateful. As well as the individuals named, I would like to thank the Islamic Art and Material Culture SSN UK for its support of the project, and the sixth form of the Royal High School, Bath, who helped at the final fundraising event. For their enthusiasm and support with research for the project, our thanks are due to David Sykes, Moya Carey, Melanie Gibson, and Will Kwiatkowski. Our particular thanks to Kate Newnham and to Bristol Museum & Art Gallery for kindly allowing us to quote from Miss Tanner's journal.

It is wonderful that by reviving Miss Tanner's collection we are able to broaden the cultural diversity of our displays and, through it, to speak to a wider variety of audiences. Thank you again to everybody who has contributed in any way.

CHRIS STEPHENS
DIRECTOR

Bath to Baghdad

Ellen Tanner first visited the Middle East in late 1894. She set off from Victoria Station for Marseilles, took a merchant steamer through the Red Sea, Gulf of Aden and Persian Gulf to Iraq (then known as Mesopotamia) and up the River Tigris to Baghdad, followed by a circular route overland through Iran (then called Persia), before returning to Baghdad (see map printed on the inside cover). Miss Tanner was an unusually intrepid woman: she travelled across Iran on horseback, with local guides as her sole companions. In her late forties she had discovered a love of travel, and sought to collect interesting examples of the wares that were sold in the bazaars of Shiraz, Isfahan and Kerman along the way. She had not intended to travel to Iran on this first trip to the region, but it turned out to be the first of three visits she would make and the start of an important and unusual collection of Persian art. She went on to donate the textiles, metalwork, lacquer and ceramics collected on her travels to museums in Bath, where she eventually settled.

Miss Ellen Georgiana Tanner FRGS (1847–1937) was the elder daughter of William Tanner, a wealthy attorney-at-law with shipping interests. The family lived at Frenchay House, just outside Bristol. Miss Tanner's mother had died when Ellen was a child, and she spent much of her adult life caring for her father.

Tent panel, hand-printed on cotton, Iran, 19th century. T13, given by Miss E.G. Tanner in 1927.

On his death in 1887, Ellen Tanner and her sister each inherited the sum of £18,000, while their two brothers received the shipping and business interests. She then proceeded to travel throughout Europe and beyond to Egypt and Turkey, before beginning her journey to Iraq and Iran. Herbert Rushton Sykes (1870–1952) would later describe her as 'having during the previous sixteen years of almost constant travel, visited nearly all the corners of the globe'.

Ellen Tanner in 1903 in Mahun, photograph by Herbert Sykes. Sykes Family Collection.

It was on this first trip to Iran that Miss Tanner collected many of the items now in the Holburne Museum's collection. We are lucky enough to have an account of this journey in her own words: Miss Tanner wrote *By Road and River: Journal of Journeys in Persia and Mesopotamia*, using the notes she took en route and compiled once she returned to Baghdad. Her wry sense of humour shines through the pages of her journal (a copy of which is held by Bristol Museum & Art Gallery), as she describes her impressions of towns, sights, art and people she encountered.

Even her opening paragraph hints at the scale of this huge journey: she went direct

> by a cargo steamer from Marseilles … rather than … by one of the Messageries Français or P. and O. steamers, [and] have the trouble of changing at Aden, & then at Karrachi, in addition to the two inevitable transhipments in the Persian Gulf and Tigris.

Her route through the Suez Canal went unremarked, and next the merchant steamer passed Obock, Muscat, Bandar Abbas, and finally Bushire (Bandar Bushehr). Tanner was travelling with a friend, Emma Mockler, wife of the British Resident at Baghdad, which was their initial destination. They proceeded up the river Tigris via Bussorah (Basra), and finally

> as we came in sight of Baghdad it looked like a fairy city with the palm-fringed river, orange gardens, the houses on the water side like Venice, and all her mosques and minarets gleaming in the yellow evening sunlight.

Miss Tanner remained at the British Residency exploring the city and planning her Persian journey for several months before setting off in March 1895 back down the Tigris to the Persian port of Bandar Bushehr, at the start of the caravan route to Teheran, Isfahan, Shiraz and central Persia.

Empire in the late nineteenth century

The lands Miss Tanner referred to as Persia (which became Iran in 1925 after the fall of the Qajar dynasty) and Mesopotamia (which became Iraq in 1932) held great strategic importance for the British Empire. The late nineteenth century saw the Middle East, Iran in particular, become a focus of diplomatic attention. Britain invested in a vast programme to improve the infrastructure of the telegraph system, enabling communication across the British Empire as far as India. Iran was an important trade partner, and as well as seeking trade advantages Britain flooded the market with its own exports of textiles, metals and other industrial products, which had a direct effect on Persia's own finances at a time of great upheaval under the Qajar dynasty (1785–1925). Miss Tanner even notes that 'the bazaars at Bushire, Bussorah, and Baghdad are full of Manchester goods'. It was not only Britain that vied for power in these lands: Russian and Turkish policies of trade and expansion, and wider European upheavals, had a major impact on Iran's economy and development.

Women travellers

Miss Tanner was among the first British women to travel solo around the Middle East. Gertrude Bell had first gone to Iran in 1892 to see her uncle Sir Frank Lascelles, who was posted to Teheran. Isabella Bird

The Europeans at Yazd, 1903, photograph by Herbert Sykes. Sykes Family Collection. Ellen Tanner is fifth from left.

travelled there in 1890 with Major Herbert Sawyer. On a visit to a mission outside Jolfa, near Isfahan, Miss Tanner met 'Miss Bird (a cousin of the celebrated traveller of that name)'. Ella Sykes would accompany her brother, Percy Molesworth Sykes, who set up the consulate at Kerman in 1895. Miss Tanner was unusual in not being attached to a husband or brother with an official position.

It is surprising that Miss Tanner is so little known as a pioneering traveller to the region: she was well connected and knew and travelled with important figures of the time. She notes that

> this highly interesting, and to most people entirely new part of the World in spite of its ancient splendour of civilization and tradition, must to women at least remain inaccessible, unless like me they are fortunate enough to have connections or friends in Mesopotamia who can and will put them up, for hotels there are none.

Her own connections allowed her to stay at the British residencies or legations (embassies) in Baghdad and

Teheran. She had letters of introduction from friends and acquaintances along her route. She would later travel with members of the Sykes family, and was given two tiles by Percy Sykes (see page 38).

Miss Tanner was elected Fellow of the Royal Geographical Society in June 1913. Although women had in 1892 been permitted to join as fellows (and Isabella Bird was elected during this window), this was rescinded the following year and only in 1913 were women formally allowed to join following a twenty-year campaign. Miss Tanner joined during that first year, with a group of seven other women admitted at the June meeting chaired by Lord Curzon.

Miss Tanner's journeys to the Middle East

Miss Tanner had clearly engaged with the travel literature of her day. In common with other contemporary writers, she refers to Sir John Chardin's account of his travels and experiences in the Safavid era (1501–1736), *Travels in Persia* (1673–77), and the 'lively ... eminently readable' Jeanne Dieulafoy (a pioneering archaeologist whose husband was buying Persian art for the Louvre). Her most frequently cited source is George Curzon, whose *Persia and the Persian Question* (1892) would have been the most recent account of the region's geography, history, architecture and customs. Miss Tanner describes it as 'the best guide book one could desire to have ... it was never out of my hands on this journey': she carried this large, two-volume book on the often arduous journey, studying it closely, showing plates from it to people she encountered, and occasionally taking delight in correcting it, particularly when it came to the distances covered, though she attributes

Ellen Tanner (right) visiting a new telegraph line at Khabutur Khana, with Percy Sykes (back left), Ethel Sykes (centre), 1903, photograph by Herbert Sykes. Sykes Family Collection.

this to the fact that short cuts are 'not feasible with a string of baggage animals or a *takt-i-rewan* (litter)'.

Where Miss Tanner's account touches on politics, there is a sense that she was returning to Curzon's account for guidance, as their views are similar.

> The Residents on the Persian Gulf and at Baghdad have to uphold our prestige in the eyes of the Turks, Arabs and Persians, who, like all Orientals, attach great importance to externals ... the Resident at Bushire therefore has a sepoy guard, supplied by the government of India ... he is, in fact, the visible emblem of the British Empire and guardian of our political and trading interests.

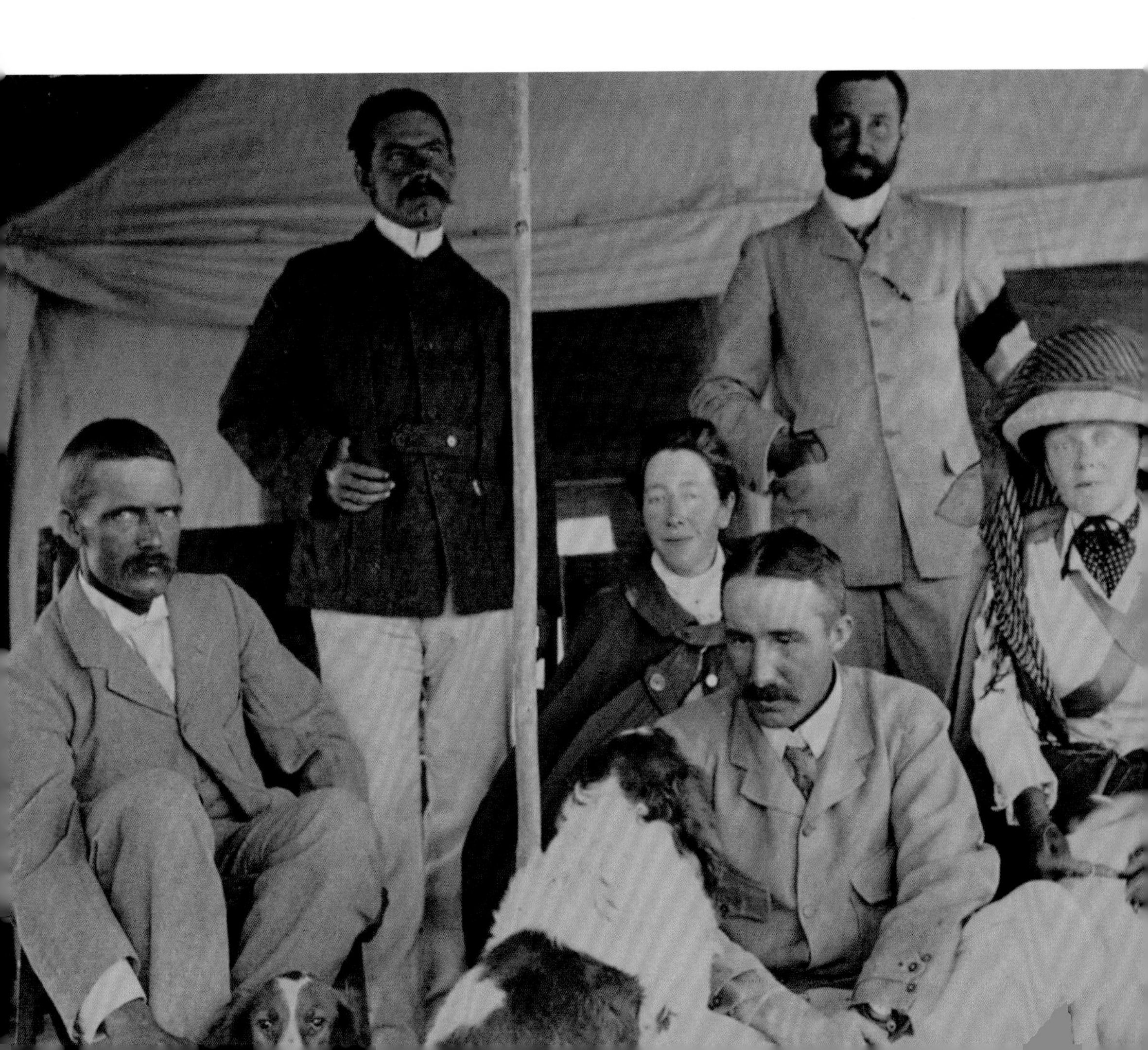

Miss Tanner's account of her journey offers insights into life as a woman travelling alone and the practicalities of covering such great distances. It is in many ways typical of British travel writing of this era: there are frequent references to horses, her saddle and the inadequacy of Persian horses unless trained by a European. On her journey through Iran Tanner was accompanied by local guides Yusef and Hannah, who were Chaldean Christians (Assyrian Catholics). The heat was so extreme that most travel was undertaken at night, and so she would arrive early in the morning at each stop along the route, set up camp, and then, as it began to cool, explore the locality.

She would normally stay in caravanserais, which ranged from the well-cared-for to the derelict: 'the Ahmidi caravanserai was large, and one of that superior sort that has in the middle of each side of the square, upper rooms, accessible by a ladder-like stair.' Where there was no suitable room, she stayed in a tent she had borrowed from her friends in Baghdad:

> It was built in the usual way: a quadrilateral entered by an arched gateway, the recesses or rooms all around, about eight feet x six, I suppose, and raised about three feet from the ground. To secure privacy the plan ensued is to hang a carpet, shawl or any sort of curtain one might possess just above the level of one's head, and there was one's bedroom!

An alternative was to stay in a telegraph house, 'one of the usual wine-bin like compartments, the key … only given up to telegraph officials, and Europeans travelling'.

Miss Tanner's own appearance did not go unremarked by the people she met.

> The women in particular chattering among themselves and pointing to the fashion of my garments as a marvel, and as I doubt not, a scandal, for I was in a cotton shirt and dark skirt, and on my head had a rather battered old sailor hat, with a blue gossamer veil to protect my eyes from the sun and dust.

She describes the importance of being protected from the sun. She often wore a solar topee, and rode 'in the thick skirt of an old hunting habit, boots and knickerbockers, and a white washing silk shirt … I had also '59 gauntlet Hexham tan gloves as unless well and thickly covered, one's hands get terribly blistered with the sun, and cause one great discomfort.'

Tea at Nasrullah Khan's house, 1903, photograph by Herbert Sykes. Sykes Family Collection. Ellen Tanner is on the left.

To go around the bazaars, she adopted the Persian *chadar*, a head-to-foot cover of black silk or black glazed calico, which at times afforded her some anonymity:

> After a rest and some food, I put on my disguising Persian clothes, as I wanted to explore Yezdikhast without being crowded round by the curious inhabitants ... doubtless the people perceived I was a Feringhee [foreigner] from my walk, as I cannot attain to the Persian shuffle; but being veiled duly, and bundled up in the chadar, and full baggy trousers all Persian women wear, I presented nothing to shock and astonish their eyes, and passed unimpeded on my way.

There were places she could not go as a woman, but there is little sense that she felt vulnerable, and along the road other travellers asked to journey with her for the protection that her caravan, as a European, would afford them. She could not enter the mosques, although in Baghdad, thanks to 'an enlightened Mahommedan gentleman close by ... from his roof top we looked over the Mosque, which for beauty I still think the finest I have ever seen, so exquisite are its proportions'.

Being a woman, however, allowed her to visit other women in private contexts. Her descriptions of women's dress offers a fascinating insight into Persian attire:

> I saw something of Persian interior life there also, my hostess taking me into some of the *anderuns* [harem, or women's area of the house]. The anderun dress of Persian women of the upper classes is ugly, and indecent, being an exaggerated ballet costume.... The regulation length of a fashionable woman's skirt in Shiraz, I was told, is the span of the wearer's hand and the width of her four fingers laid together, and, judging from those I saw, I quite believed it, and the amount of bare skin visible was great.

(*above*) Embroidered top, silk, cotton and sequins, Iran, 19th century. T31A&B, given by Miss E.G. Tanner in 1928.

(right) Teacup, enamel on copper. Iran, 19th century. C844L, given by Miss E.G. Tanner in 1928.

'Never by any possibility could I experience greater or more delightful hospitality and kindness than I met with in Persia.' Any visit would be preceded by sending ahead gifts to the host, followed by an elaborate tea, consisting of trays of sweetmeats, sherbet (a refreshing flavoured drink; see page 33), and sweet tea. 'Afternoon tea in Persia is accompanied by cucumbers and piles of fresh lettuce, of which the company eat freely, dipping the lettuce into little glasses which have a mixture of honey and vinegar in them.' Taking tea was a lengthy affair and an opportunity for conversation, and Miss Tanner often commented on what Persian women made of her:

> The questions they asked about me were endless, and always the same, such as Why had I come? and What next did I mean to do? Why was I not married? and How did I put my clothes on? All asked with a great show of interest, and much laughter and merriment.

Miss Tanner's diet on the road consisted of such teas or dinners whenever she was hosted, but the food taken on the journey consisted mostly of tinned food, dry biscuits and boiled milk, and arrowroot (used to make a pudding similar to tapioca), and occasionally laudanum and brandy when she became sick from the water. By the end of her journey through Iran and Iraq, she had lost three stone.

An important pastime on the route was visiting the bazaars. Although Miss Tanner does not explicitly discuss the impetus behind her purchases, she was clearly buying on a large scale.

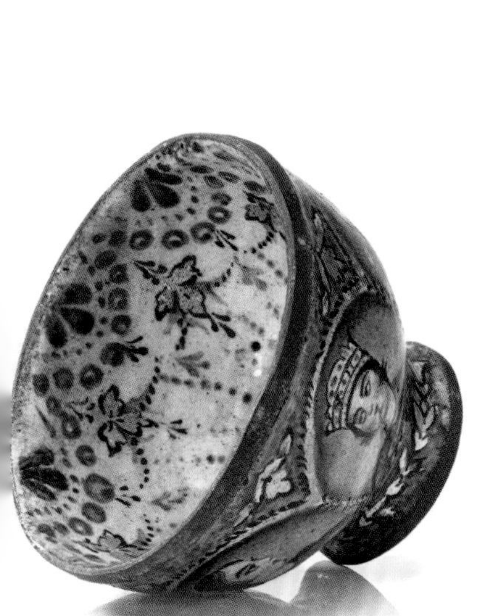

> Here are carpets, shawls from Kerman, silks from Yezd, and in fact all the best productions of the country, and often I regretted afterwards that I had

> not made more purchases at Shiraz, instead of waiting for Teheran, where the market is dearer, and it is becoming increasingly difficult to get hold of good things.

Her account offers insights into some of the practicalities of travel and forming a collection. Tanner relied on agents to transport the items she had brought home, with mixed success: 'though I entrusted the packing to the Persian Gulf Trading company, it arrived in London in a wrecked state.' This may account for some of the old repairs on items now in the Holburne's collection, such as the rivets holding together a Chinese jar bought in Baghdad in 1896. The remoteness of the desert regions comes through repeatedly, along with a sense of how long it takes for communications to reach people: she talks of lost letters, and expresses her great relief to see fellow countrymen along the way, if only for the conversation, as she could not speak Persian and only communicated with Persians in French if they spoke it.

Many of her reflections on Persians and Persian life read as extraordinarily superior and dismissive, a trait she shared with many of her British contemporaries, referring to the 'terrible immorality of the Persians'. When being taken around Kermanshah by Hadji Abdur Rhaman, a cultured ex-diplomat who served in London and Europe, she writes,

> I really pitied the poor man, trotting me round in this manner. Of course to the oriental mind one is mad to move about in the heat of the day, and go hither and thither looking at antiquities and places of no interest to the native.

Book cover, lacquer and leather, Iran (Isfahan), 19th century. E203, given by Miss E.G. Tanner in 1920.

She describes with typical frankness her attitude to religions she is not fully engaged with:

> I am told it is far better to profess Christianity in Persia than to be a Suni Mahommedan, as the Persians are all bigoted Shiahs, and regard the Sunis much as an extreme ritualist of the Anglican church does an evangelical or a dissenter.

Her humanity does come through: she expresses concern about the work of missionaries in the region, who are celebrating the conversion of an epileptic woman, 'divorced from her husband as a bad bargain', but Miss Tanner is concerned that to renounce Islam is on pain of death, and worries for the woman's life.

Collecting the arts of Persia for museums

Ellen Tanner's gifts to the Holburne Museum reflect a moment of great interest in the production and dissemination of Persian art. British collectors and museums were actively acquiring Persian art, and many of the individuals undertaking this work also had official posts. Robert Murdoch Smith, the director of the Persian Telegraph Department in Teheran, in 1873 became an agent for the South Kensington (later Victoria and Albert) Museum, which from the 1870s was actively collecting the best of the world's art for Britain's craftsmen to study. Murdoch Smith made important acquisitions for the Museum, some of which were aided by his relationship with the Qajar ruler Nasir al-Din Shah (1831–1896).

Perhaps these efforts inspired Ellen Tanner to give her collection to local museums. She was an early donor to the newly founded Bristol Museum &

Mirror case (interior), lacquer, Iran, second half of 19th century. F65B, given by Miss E.G. Tanner in 1926.

Art Gallery, giving a collection primarily of textiles and dress in 1907, and in 1927 she gave to the Bath Royal Literary and Scientific Institution a collection of 'Persian curios', including a miniature silvered samovar set (which speaks of the Russian influence in the region) and a pair of dolls. She also gave a carpet to the V&A. The fact that her gifts were given to the Holburne Museum some time after her adventures in the Middle East suggests that the collections were displayed in her homes at Parkside in Corsham, Wiltshire (where she was living in 1913); Cavendish Place, Bath (her home until 1916); and later the Lansdowne Grove Hotel.

The collection

Miss Tanner gave eighty-five objects to the Holburne as a series of gifts between 1917 and 1932, often with specific information about when and where she acquired them, reflecting the breadth of Persian craft she encountered. The majority of the material bought by Miss Tanner represented contemporary production made by craftspeople working in a local tradition and sold at bazaars. The contents of each gift are carefully recorded in the Holburne's accessions registers, and many are accompanied by original handwritten labels which state that she bought most on her first trip to Iran (see page 25). The labels, however, were clearly written some time after the trip, once she was settled in Bath, and occasionally details are vague: 'bought by the donor in Central Persia in 189_'.

The collection is striking in its variety. Textile traditions are particularly well represented, with a signed piece of silk from Kerman (see page 44), printed cottons and a great variety of traditional embroidery (see pages 34–7).

> I told Yusef to ask one of the chief silk merchants to send me some specimens of Kashan silk weaving, and embroideries for me to inspect at my leisure, and returned after two or three hours sight-seeing delighted with Kashan, which I think Mr. Curzon speaks too disparagingly of.

Tanner's account gives clear insight into the specific craft skills of particular towns. We learn that in Karbala the makers were producing replicas of architectural tiles, which may assist with dating some tiles (including our tile, F54, left): 'We spent a happy hour at a tile maker, where I ordered some to be made for me by the Persian makers after patterns of some old ones taken off the mosques.' In Shiraz, Miss Tanner bought examples of hammered metalwork, like the mirror (see page 43). Isfahan, the old Safavid capital, was still known for its metalworking and steel traditions (see pages 30 & 40); Abadeh was known for its elaborately carved pearwood (see page 32); Yezd for its textiles and marble, 'very beautiful, each step being a solid block of the most lovely semi-translucent marble, faintly tinged with pinkish yellow tones. Nowhere, not even in Athens, have I seen marble of more exquisite colour.'

Murdoch Smith differed from many of his contemporaries in making a strong case for the importance of Qajar art in itself, rather than as a less accomplished descendant of the great artistic output of the period of Moghul emperor Shah Jahan (1592–1666) or the artistic flourishing during the Safavid era (1501–1736). His book *Persian Art* (1877) is an in-depth study of the arts of Iran at the end of the nineteenth century, making the case that the arts of Persia were not declining or

Tile with floral decoration, Iran, late 19th century. F54, given by Miss E.G. Tanner in 1926.

dead. What is extraordinary, given that the V&A was actively collecting, is that parts of the Iranian collection acquired by Smith and illustrated in his book were later deaccessioned (particularly the metalwork, which is a highlight of Tanner's collection). This makes the survival of Tanner's collections at the Holburne and the textiles at Bristol Museum even more important.

Although Tanner paid for the items she acquired from the bazaars, clearly she is also implicated in the wholesale purchasing of historic artefacts in Iran at this time. As the Qajar government took action under pressure from religious groups regarding the removal of tiles from buildings, Murdoch Smith began to give less specific provenances. The historic tiles from the Holburne's collection (see pages 38–9) tell us something of that story. On one occasion Tanner bought items from a tomb that had just been excavated in Hamedan, and once took tiles from a site:

> from the ruined palace adjoining the Aineh-Khaneh I abstracted three tiles from a small inner chamber leading into the bath. I was ashamed of myself for this act of vandalism, but it seemed to me seeing how these beautiful tiles were suffered to fall off and lie neglected on the ground, that they would be better appreciated by me than by the Persians.

Miss Tanner's legacy

What makes Ellen Tanner's collection extraordinary is not the overall quality of the individual pieces (although there are items of great beauty and rarity) but the fact that this collection exists at all. Until recently the only part of Miss Tanner's collection visible to the public was a seventeenth-century tile panel from

Damascus: others were in store and in urgent need of conservation. This exhibition and conservation project reveal a previously unexplored part of the Holburne Museum's story in all its eclecticism: like Sir William Holburne's collection, it is about the work of individuals, formed through a lifetime of exploration, and remains largely intact for us to rediscover today. Ellen Tanner was both a pioneering woman and a supporter of Empire; an impassioned collector and enthusiast, and an appropriator of Persian artistic culture.

There is an additional poignancy in Miss Tanner's evocative descriptions of places that in recent years have been more familiar to us for the turmoil taking place there than for their extraordinary history and culture: 'The palm-fringed banks, the shipping, the creeks, and above all the dazzling sun-light of Bussorah [Basra] charmed me.' Many of these places felt as distant to a traveller then as today. Ellen Tanner gave to the Holburne Museum collections from Syria and from Iraq. That these objects are now in Bath highlights both the interest in the world that travelling can inspire and the fragility of cultural heritage. It is a salient reminder of Britain's past involvement, much of it less than exemplary, in international affairs, and a chance to celebrate the extraordinary artistic and cultural output of the Islamic world.

HIGHLIGHTS OF THE COLLECTION

Playing cards

Lacquer, Iran, 19th century. F84. Given by Miss E.G. Tanner in 1927.

These cards were used to play *As-Nas*, a game which formed the basis of modern poker. In her journal, Miss Tanner describes the game: 'It is played by 4 persons, each player receiving 5 cards. Dealt from left to right one at a time.' A full set would contain five of each card, often with variations in the design, even within the same pack. The suits, however, were standard: an *As* or Ace, represented as a lion fighting a dragon; a *Serbaz* (soldier); a *Shah* (king); a *Bibi* (queen); and a *Couli* (dancer). The cards are made from papier mâché, onto which the decoration has been hand-painted. Over this a layer of lacquer has been added, which protects the paint and gives the cards their shiny finish. Lacquering became a popular production technique for small decorative objects, especially during the rule of the Qajar dynasty (1785–1925). Later examples reflect the influence of European design, a result of increasing trade with Europe. The dress of the *Couli* reflects the later nineteenth-century taste for shorter flared skirts.

Painting on glass

Glass, pigment, wood, Iran, late 19th century. M183. Given by Miss E.G. Tanner in 1926.

These young lovers in an interior are shown in wonderful detail, from their carefully rendered dress to the patterned carpet and fretwork of their seat. The highlights and details were painted on the back of the glass first, building up layer by layer. Tanner's notes describe the unsigned portrait as representing 'Shah Abbas and a wife'. This is highly unlikely: Shah Abbas (Safavid ruler of Iran 1571–1629) was usually rendered with a distinctive long moustache and turban, and the painting style suggests a much later date. This young man wears a Qajar-style cap and woven silk jacket. The woman's outfit includes voluminous printed or embroidered trousers with a *pirahan* or chemise. On the reverse of the frame is handwritten 'Reuter Collection'. This may refer to Baron Julius de Reuter, who in 1872 signed an agreement with Nasir al-Din Shah which gave Reuter control over all roads, telegraphs and industrial production in Persia, including profits, for twenty years. This unpopular agreement was short-lived, and Reuter went on to found the Imperial Bank of Persia.

Mirror case

Lacquer, Iran, 19th century. F65B. Given by Miss E.G. Tanner in 1926.

The decoration on this lacquer mirror frame comes from Firdawsi's *Shahnama*, or *Book of Kings*, the mythical account of the history of Iran.

On one side (left) we see the moment when King Khosrow first catches sight of Shirin, whom he will later marry, bathing. On the other side (right) Farhad, the humble engineer and craftsman famed for his skill at carving rock, catches sight of Shirin, by then Queen of Armenia, on horseback and falls in love. Inside, a floral motif (page 20) reflects the popularity of European flower painting in Iran and the exchange of design ideas since the seventeenth century.

The frame does not contain a mirror; Miss Tanner describes buying mirrors when she returned home, probably due to the risk of breaking the glass in the long transit.

Peacock & hawk

Steel with inlaid gold and silver decoration, Iran (Isfahan), 19th century. F131 & F73. Given by Miss E.G. Tanner in 1932 & 1927.

Animal figures like these birds were often attached to the *'alam*, or standard, carried in the mourning processions of *Muharram*, the Iranian New Year. Deer and lions and a variety of birds, particularly the peacock and fantail pigeon, were particularly popular. Miss Tanner watched one of these processions when she was staying in Gulahek, near Teheran, in the summer of 1895.

The gold and silver inlay is characteristic of traditional Persian steel. The effect is produced using a sharp, short-edged knife to incise the surface. Very fine gold or silver wire is placed on the roughened surface and hammered in. The surface is then polished with agate, which brings the silver and gold to a shine.

The peacock has an important role in Persian and Sufi iconography. It was also a key motif in Shah Jahan's Peacock Throne, which Miss Tanner elected not to visit when she was in Teheran, as 'Mr. Curzon says it is an imposter'.

The Holburne's peacock originally had a fanned tail, probably of pierced metal, which has been lost.

Box & sherbet ladles

Carved pearwood, Iran (Abadeh), 19th century. F71 & F72. Given by Miss E.G. Tanner in 1927.

The city of Abadeh was known for its carved pearwood. Tanner set out to buy some examples when she visited: 'Here I got some of the pear-wood carving eulogized so highly by Mr. Curzon, and interviewed the best wood worker in the place. The work is excessively delicate … done with a common small knife; the wood whittled down to a paper-like thinness; the bowls semi-transparent, and the handles carved in wonderful and intricate designs. It seemed almost incredible that such results could be attained with such rude implements.'

These ladles would have been used to serve sherbet, a refreshing fruit-based drink. Miss Tanner describes the often elaborate experience of taking tea in Persia: 'We found the lady seated in state expecting us, sherbet in a handsome china bowl with a beautiful ladle of the delicately carved Abadeh pear wood work to serve it with, sweet meats, and pale, excessively sweet tea in small glasses. All this on the carpet, set out on trays before her.'

The box is carved with foliage, flowers and birds, with on the lid a central motif showing a lion fighting a dragon. Miss Tanner's handwritten label (illustrated page 25) tells us this is a 'carved copy of the bas-reliefs at Persepolis', although it is not a direct copy as the surviving motif at Persepolis shows a lion fighting a bull. This imagery represents a life and death struggle for the strength and power of the monarchy; it appears in much Iranian art and can also be found on the *As-Nas* playing cards (page 26).

Purses

Silk, cotton and sequins, Iran, 19th century. T29ABC & T30. Given by Miss E.G. Tanner in 1928.

Small purses and samples of different types of embroidery form a significant part of Miss Tanner's collection at the Holburne Museum. These brightly coloured drawstring purses are embellished with embroidery and sequins, and covered with fine netting. The netting might have been an original design feature (some of the netting is itself embellished with foil and sequins), or added to protect the embroidery and sequins underneath. The square purse on the right is referred to as a *bokhcha*, used to carry pages of a Quran.

Embroidered shawl

Wool and silk, Iran (Kerman), 19th century. T12. Given by Miss E.G. Tanner in 1927.

A great variety of Persian textiles were produced in Kerman. This technique is called *pateh-duzi*, and involves fine wool, sometimes combined with silk, elaborately embroidered freehand. It is characterized by rows of small squares or boxes outlining the motifs, and a pattern consisting of a central medallion and *boteh*, or paisley, motifs in the four corners. The thick embroidery and rectangular shape of this shawl suggest it was not for wearing, but was probably for use as a table cover. Miss Tanner may have bought this in Shiraz, where many Kerman wares were sold, on her first visit, or when she visited Kerman on her third visit to Iran in 1903.

Persian Needlework
Box bought in
Central Persia in
1896 by

Needlework box & trouser panel

Silk and cotton, Iran, 19th century. F79 & T24. Given by Miss E.G. Tanner in 1928.

This embroidered trouser panel and needlework box are examples of Naksh (or *naqšeh*) embroidery, most commonly produced in Isfahan and Yazd, but also in Shiraz and Kashan. Several panels of embroidery would be sewn together to make women's trousers. These intricate designs are made by creating a framework of diagonal lines and filling in the floral motifs using tent stitch in colourful silk or cotton threads, until the entire surface is covered with embroidery. The needlework box has been made from a piece of repurposed trouser panel and sold as a decorative item in its own right. Miss Tanner's handwritten label inside the lid of the box reads 'Persian Needlework box bought in Central Persia in 1896 by EG Tanner'. The box is lined with a printed glazed fabric. The reverse of the panel (below) shows how the once vivid colours have faded with time and light exposure.

Two tiles

Fritware with *cuerda seca* decoration, 1425–75. F55&A. Given by Miss E.G. Tanner in 1926.

These tiles once formed part of the decoration of a madrasah (religious college) in the town of Khargird in north-eastern Iran. Miss Tanner did not visit the site while she was in Iran: she was given the tiles by Percy Molesworth Sykes (1967–1945), who bought them at a bazaar in Mashhad while he was based at the consulate there.

Miss Tanner was in the country at almost the same time as Ella Sykes, who first accompanied her brother to the region in 1895, and later wrote an account of her trip, *Through Persia on a Side-Saddle.* Although Tanner does not mention the Sykes family in her journal, she later travelled with Ella, Ethel and Herbert Sykes, and appears in a family photograph album from their trip to Iran in 1903–4.

The technique used to create the multicoloured pattern is known as *cuerda seca*, using wax (which burns away) to keep the coloured pigments from running into each other during firing. The tiles still have traces of their original gold-leaf decoration.

Tile

Fritware with moulded, overglazed and gilded decoration, Iran (Takht-i Sulaiman), about 1275. C927A136X. Given by Miss E.G. Tanner in 1920.

The decoration of this tile is known as *lajvardina* ('lapis lazuli'), which refers to the distinctive combination of blue and gold. It is the earliest artefact in the collection, and is a very rare form showing a leaping animal. It was made for Takht-i Sulaiman (Throne of Solomon), a hunting palace built by the Mongol ruler Abaqa Khan (1265–1282) on a site which had previously had the remains of a Zoroastrian fire temple built during the Sassanid period (224–651). Many tiles were removed from the Takht-i Sulaiman complex, and possibly reused on other buildings, long before the nineteenth century when there was great Western interest in Middle Eastern tiles. Only ruins of the site remain today, but remnants of many different decoration types and techniques were found, including lustre-glazed tiles in star and geometric shapes, tiles depicting Chinese motifs such as the dragon and the phoenix, and inscription bands with verses from the *Shahnama*, the national epic of Persia. Miss Tanner described the tile as coming 'from a tomb at Hamadan, Iran' when she gave it to the Holburne Museum, but it is not clear whether she knew its earlier origin.

Vases

Pierced and chased brass, Iran, 19th century. F66A, F66B, F66C. Given by Miss E.G. Tanner in 1926.

Miss Tanner describes seeing the metalwork the bazaars at Kashan: 'I put on my Persian outdoor costume, and went to see the bazaars … these are finer, I consider, than those at Isfahan, though less extensive, and the merchandise in them better worth looking at; really good brass and copper work being done there, and silk weaving.' Typically, she suggests the declining quality of modern Persian metalwork: 'Neither did I see any of the pierced and inlaid brass-work spoken of by [Curzon], and was told that this was peculiar to Isfahan, where it is in quantities, and very handsome and artistic, though the modern work is by no means equal to the old there.'

The large size and detailed design of these pierced and chased brass vases make them very unusual. The designs incorporate arabesque designs known as *eslimi* and Quranic inscriptions that have become so stylized they are no longer recognizable as script. The smaller vase (left) features half-man, half-animal figures, representing the life-and-death struggle of the Iranian monarch with an animal, symbolizing the evil forces of the world. The motifs are found at Persepolis, one of the seasonal capitals of the Achaemenid rulers of the ancient Persian Empire (550–330 BCE).

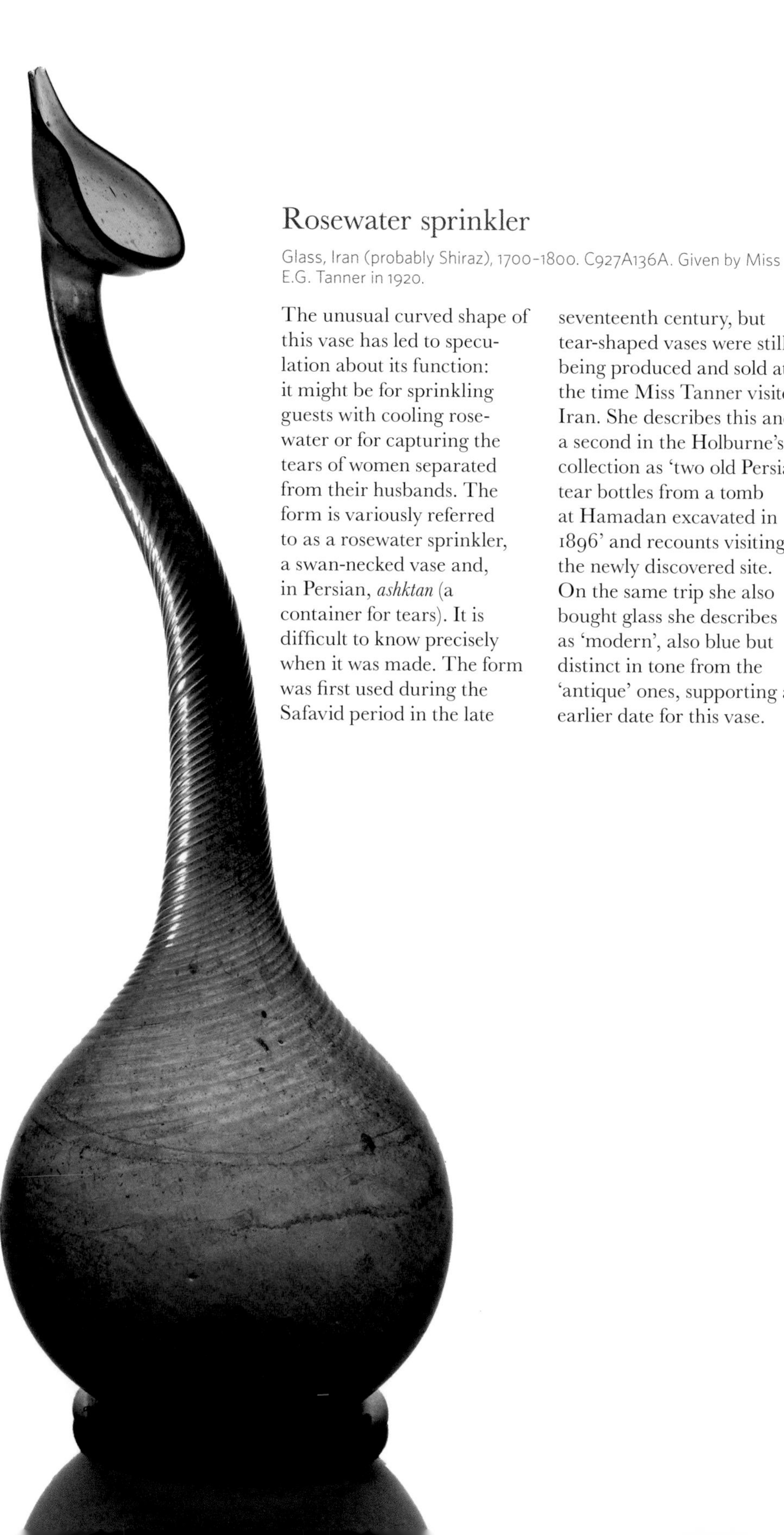

Rosewater sprinkler

Glass, Iran (probably Shiraz), 1700–1800. C927A136A. Given by Miss E.G. Tanner in 1920.

The unusual curved shape of this vase has led to speculation about its function: it might be for sprinkling guests with cooling rosewater or for capturing the tears of women separated from their husbands. The form is variously referred to as a rosewater sprinkler, a swan-necked vase and, in Persian, *ashktan* (a container for tears). It is difficult to know precisely when it was made. The form was first used during the Safavid period in the late seventeenth century, but tear-shaped vases were still being produced and sold at the time Miss Tanner visited Iran. She describes this and a second in the Holburne's collection as 'two old Persian tear bottles from a tomb at Hamadan excavated in 1896' and recounts visiting the newly discovered site. On the same trip she also bought glass she describes as 'modern', also blue but distinct in tone from the 'antique' ones, supporting an earlier date for this vase.

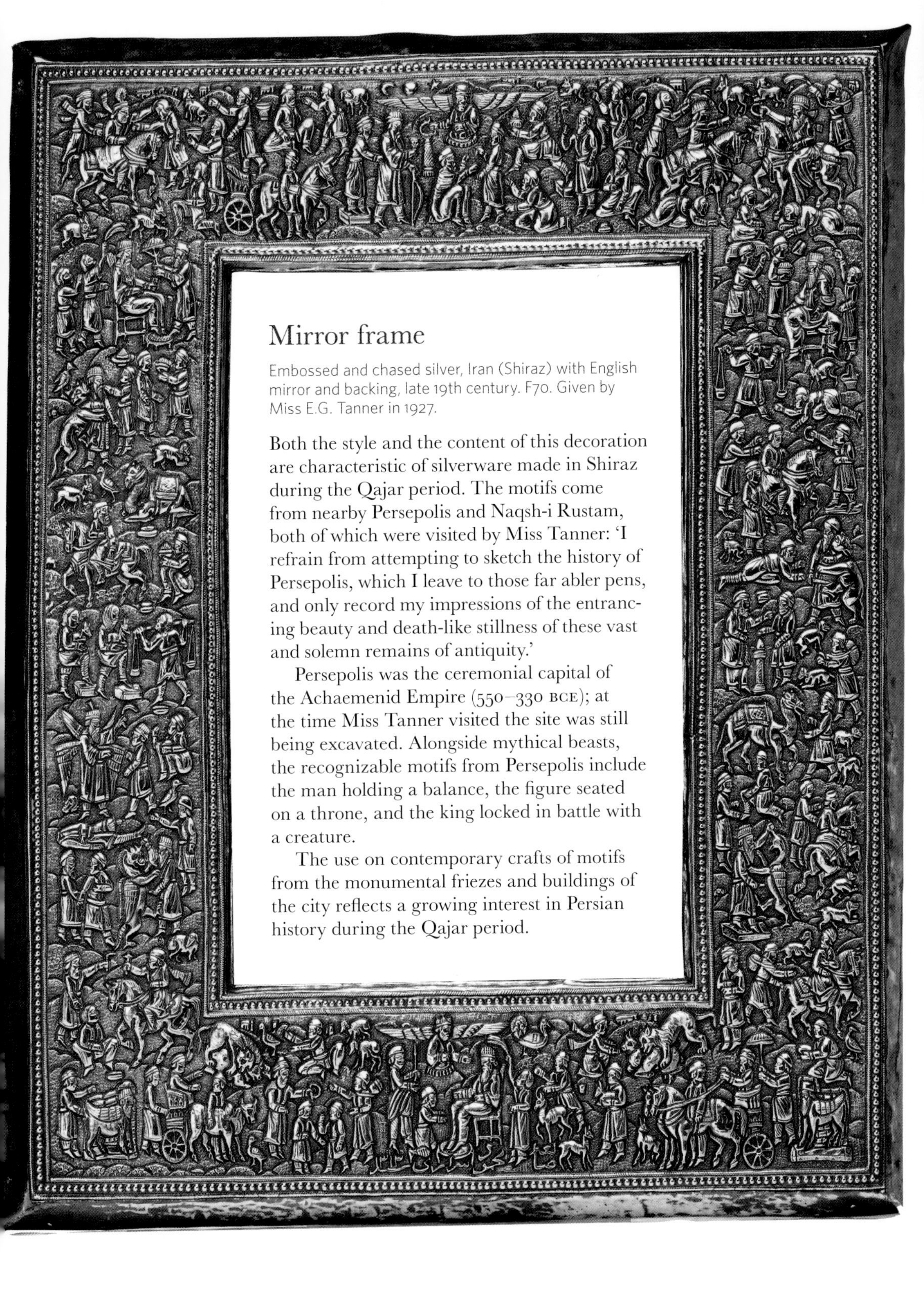

Mirror frame

Embossed and chased silver, Iran (Shiraz) with English mirror and backing, late 19th century. F70. Given by Miss E.G. Tanner in 1927.

Both the style and the content of this decoration are characteristic of silverware made in Shiraz during the Qajar period. The motifs come from nearby Persepolis and Naqsh-i Rustam, both of which were visited by Miss Tanner: 'I refrain from attempting to sketch the history of Persepolis, which I leave to those far abler pens, and only record my impressions of the entrancing beauty and death-like stillness of these vast and solemn remains of antiquity.'

Persepolis was the ceremonial capital of the Achaemenid Empire (550–330 BCE); at the time Miss Tanner visited the site was still being excavated. Alongside mythical beasts, the recognizable motifs from Persepolis include the man holding a balance, the figure seated on a throne, and the king locked in battle with a creature.

The use on contemporary crafts of motifs from the monumental friezes and buildings of the city reflects a growing interest in Persian history during the Qajar period.

Fragment of damask

Silk, Iran (Kashan), 19th century. T15.
Given by Miss E.G. Tanner in 1927.

Miss Tanner describes buying this fragment in Kashan: 'I also bought a handsome web of ivory-white silk of fine texture, with a singular damasked pattern of peacocks on it. It was roughly finished compared with Indian or European silk, but very quaint and charming, and at the end of the web was an inscription in Kufic characters, woven into the fabric, which being a dead language I could not get translated. The effect was that of a fine white damask table cloth, and I carried off my web highly delighted with it.' The selvedge has the name of the maker woven into it: Husain Kashani or Kuli-kani, one of the few makers known by name during this period.

Two vessels

Soapstone, Iran (Mashhad), 1903–4. C927A126 & 7. Given by Miss E.G. Tanner in 1920.

Miss Tanner bought these vessels in Mashhad on her third trip to Iran with Ella, Ethel and Herbert Sykes in 1903. She describes the vessel (left) as 'a Persian water bottle of Meshad slate' but it is in fact a type of soapstone, which is soft and suitable for carving and turning. It has an unusual hollow ring-shaped interior with a pierced hole at the centre, perhaps to allow air to circulate and cool the water. The ring shape may be derived from early Iranian vessels of the third century. The vase in the shape of the 'Hand of the Blessed Fatima' (right) uses iconography known in Islamic art to represent the Five Pillars of Islam: profession of faith, daily prayers, alms for the poor, fasting during Ramadan and pilgrimage to Mecca. Islamic art is rich with figural decoration: in the wall paintings and mural tiles within palaces, in manuscript illumination, on textiles and on metalwork and ceramics not intended for religious purpose. Here, the leaping lions, birds and hares are typical of late Qajar-period decoration.

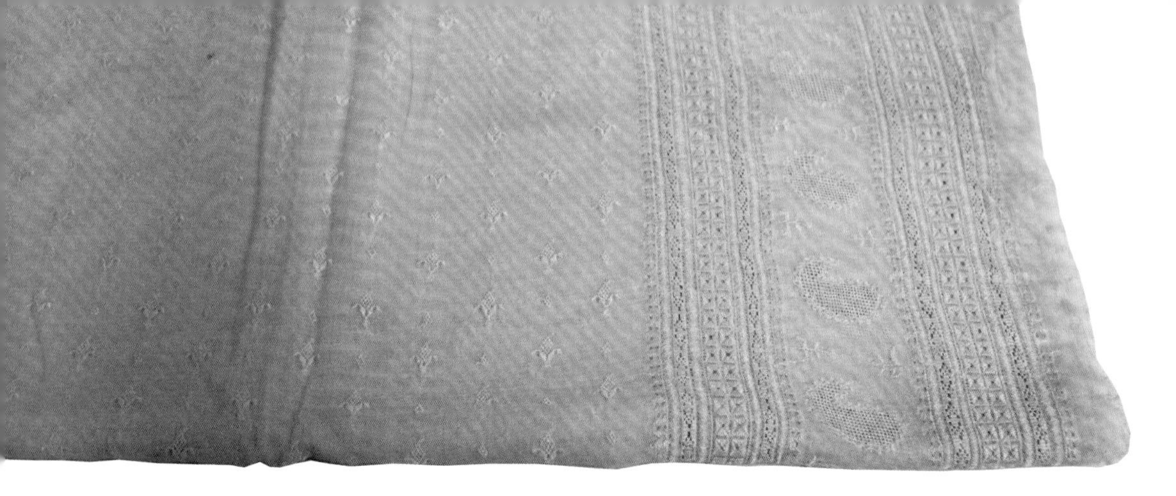

CONSERVING THE COLLECTION

Ellen Tanner's collection is on display for the first time following a major conservation project. The collection has travelled to specialist conservation studios across the country, including West Dean College, whose students have worked on them as part of their training. These meticulous conservation processes have transformed the collection.

Many of the items were not new when Miss Tanner bought them. In her journal she describes the challenges of getting objects home in one piece (see page 40) and she bought the glass for mirror frames at home in London on her return (see page 50). The goal of the conservation work was not to restore these objects to how they looked when new, but to return them to a stable condition, revealing some extraordinary details which had been obscured.

The delicate muslin shawl was washed, a process which removed staining and discolouration and restored its former white colour. Rust and corrosion that had built up on the surface of the steel peacock hid elaborate decoration. Conservators were able to remove these layers without damaging the gold and silver beneath. The peacock's tail was not so lucky: it does not seem to have survived the damp conditions in the Holburne's basement before the stores were environmentally controlled.

We had hoped to conserve 25 objects for the exhibition, but the success of the Big Give campaign enabled us to conserve 61 items. For the first time, Ellen Tanner's collection is on show, catalogued and accessible online, and we have been able to share this little-known story more widely than we had thought possible.

Published to accompany the exhibition

Bath to Baghdad: Ellen Tanner's Collection of Middle Eastern Art

14 June–21 October 2018

The Holburne Museum
Great Pulteney Street
Bath, BA2 4DB

www.holburne.org

Registered charity no. 310288

Published by The Holburne Museum

ISBN 978 0 903679 16 9

Miss Tanner's journal is unpublished. Quotations within this text are taken from a typescript held by Bristol Museum & Art Gallery with their kind permission.

All place names in the text and maps have been transliterated to the most common English usage. This is at times different from Ellen Tanner's own usage and we have given both instances where relevant.

Entries on pages 26, 33, 34 and 36 were written by Kate Vandor.

Photographs by Herbert Sykes on pages 8, 11, 13 and 15 reproduced with kind permission of David Sykes.
Photograph of shawl on page 46 © Catrin Jones.
All other photography © The Holburne Museum | www.tonygilbert.co.uk

page 2, detail from shawl, embroidered wool and silk. Iran (Kerman), 19th century. T12, given by Miss E.G. Tanner in 1927.
pages 4-5, two teacups and saucers, enamel on copper. Iran, 19th century. C844L&M, given by Miss E.G. Tanner in 1928.
page 25, detail from box, carved pearwood. Iran (Abadeh) 19th century. F72, given by Miss E.G. Tanner in 1927.

Designed and typeset in Baskerville by illuminati, Grosmont
Printed and bound in Wales by Gomer Press Limited